Foundation Paper 3a
Economics for Business

D1740087

First edition 2002
Second edition January 2003

ISBN 0 7517 0118 1 (Second edition 0 7517 3632 5)

British Library Cataloguing-in-Publication Data

A catalogue record for this book is available from the British Library

Published by

BPP Professional Education, Aldine House, Aldine Place, London W12 8AW

www.bpp.com

Printed in Great Britain by Ashford Colour Press

Welcome to BPP's CIMA **Passcards**.

- They **save you time**. Important topics are summarised for you.

- They incorporate **diagrams** to kick start your memory.

- They follow the overall **structure** of the BPP Study Texts, but BPP's CIMA **Passcards** are not just a condensed book. Each card has been separately designed for clear presentation. Topics are self contained and can be grasped visually.

- CIMA **Passcards** are still **just the right size** for pockets, briefcases and bags.

- CIMA **Passcards focus on the exam** you will be facing.

Run through the complete set of **Passcards** as often as you can during your final revision period. The day before the exam, try to go through the **Passcards** again! You will then be well on your way to passing your exams. **Good luck!**

BPP also publishes a Practice & Revision Kit and MCQ Cards, which contain lots of questions for you to attempt during your final revision period.

1: The allocation of scarce resources

Topic List

Fundamentals

The fundamental concepts of economics, such as scarcity, choice and opportunity cost are frequently the subject of multiple choice questions. You must grasp the essential nature of economics if you are to comprehend the significance of what comes later.

Economics is concerned with the production and consumption of goods and services: what to produce, how to produce it and who to produce it for.

Scarcity of resources

The production of goods and services requires the utilisation of economic **resources**. These resources are **scarce** and therefore choices must be made to how they are to be employed.

- LAND includes all **natural resources**. Land itself is limited in quantity but can be improved in quality.

- LABOUR is people employed to produce goods and services. it varies in quality.

- CAPITAL consists of physical goods that aid production. Money can be transformed into real capital.

- ENTERPRISE is needed both to organise production and to take the risk of possible financial loss.

Production possibility curve (PPC)

The PPC illustrates two important economic ideas.

- A society's total productive potential can be used to produce a wide range of possible outputs.

- Choices must be made. More of one good implies less of another if the economy is producing to its potential.

If the economy is producing at point A, more of both goods X and Y may be obtained by improved efficiency. To move from point B to point C means given up some of good X to obtain more of good Y. The **opportunity cost** of a good is the quantity of other goods that must be foregone.

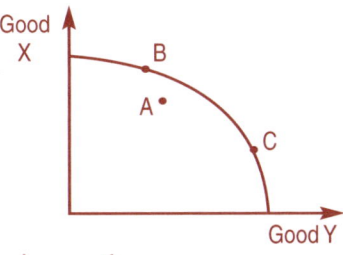

Economic growth

occurs when total productive potential capacity increases. The overall PPC moves outwards and it becomes possible to produce more goods and services of all types. For practical purposes, economic growth is measured by annual increase in national income (see Chapter 13).

Economic growth

Economic welfare

Economic welfare is primarily determined by two things.
- The level of output of goods and services
- The existence of negative externalities (see Chapter 4) such as pollution, noise and social dislocation

The distribution of output among the population is also an economic welfare issue.

Factors influencing growth

Economic growth depends on the quality and quantity of scarce resources available and the efficiency with which they are used. Technological advances; education and training; and increases in either the population or the participation rate all lead to growth.

Sustainable growth

Economic growth that exceeds the rate of population growth leads to a generally higher standard of living. However, there are problems with economic growth:
- Depletion of natural resources: are substitutes available?
- Negative externalities reduce the rate of growth of economic welfare, since they must be borne or resource used to limit their effects.
- Growth brings human problems such as unemployment.

2: The price mechanism

Topic List

The market

Demand

Supply

The price mechanism

Maximum and minimum prices

This is another chapter of fundamentals that must be understood properly. Pay particular attention to the factors other than price that affect demand and supply. These are a fruitful source of questions.

A market

Potential buyers and potential sellers come together for the purpose of exchange.

Sellers are **firms**. Buyers of consumer goods are **households.**

Utility

The pleasure or benefit or satisfaction derived from the consumption of a good. **Marginal utility** is the utility derived from the consumption of one additional unit.

Consumers are rational

- They prefer more to less.

- They will substitute one good for another if the price is right.

- They attempt to maximise total utility from a limited income.

- Marginal utility diminishes as consumption increases.

- Quantities purchased will be adjusted until their marginal utilities are equal. If this is not so, it means that the consumer would actually prefer to consume more of one good and less of another.

The demand curve

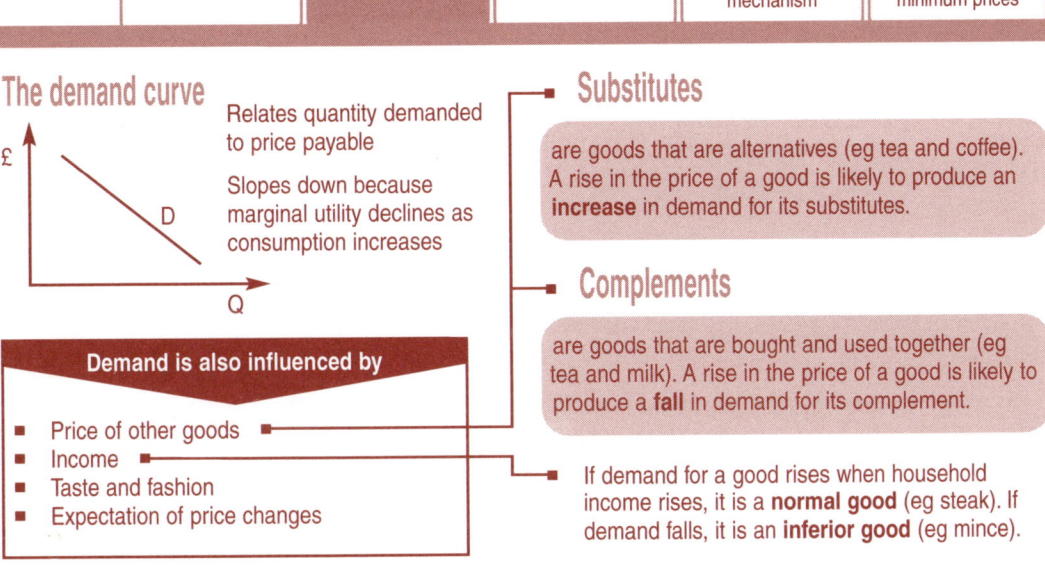

£

D

Q

Relates quantity demanded to price payable

Slopes down because marginal utility declines as consumption increases

Demand is also influenced by

- Price of other goods
- Income
- Taste and fashion
- Expectation of price changes

Substitutes

are goods that are alternatives (eg tea and coffee). A rise in the price of a good is likely to produce an **increase** in demand for its substitutes.

Complements

are goods that are bought and used together (eg tea and milk). A rise in the price of a good is likely to produce a **fall** in demand for its complement.

If demand for a good rises when household income rises, it is a **normal good** (eg steak). If demand falls, it is an **inferior good** (eg mince).

Remember! The demand curve shows how demand responds to a change in price and nothing else! Any change in the other factors that affect demand cause a shift in the position of the demand curve.

A leftward shift may be caused by

- A fall in household income
- A fall in the price of substitutes
- A rise in the price of complements
- A change in taste away from the good
- An expected fall in price

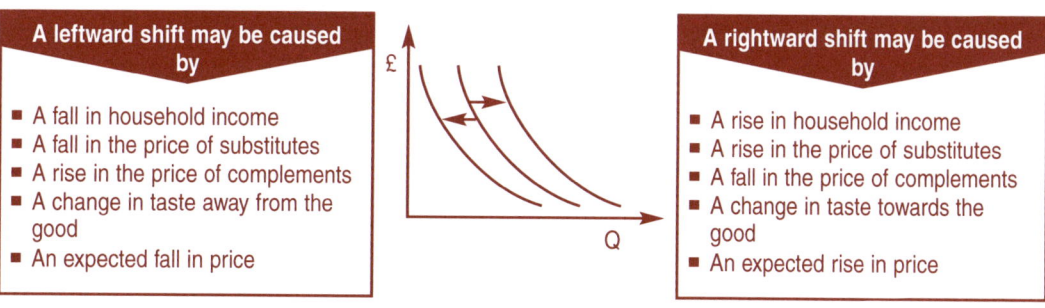

A rightward shift may be caused by

- A rise in household income
- A rise in the price of substitutes
- A fall in the price of complements
- A change in taste towards the good
- An expected rise in price

An expectation of a fall in price will lead consumers to put off their purchases in the hope of benefiting from the lower price later. An expected price rise will lead consumers to buy early and stockpile in order to avoid paying a higher price later.

The supply curve

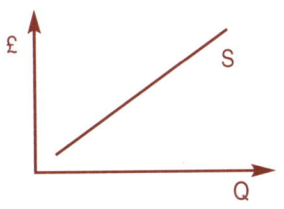

Relates quantity offered to price available.

> **Just as with demand, the effect of other factors is to cause a shift in the position of the demand curve.**

Factors influencing supply

A shift of the supply curve to the right could be caused by any of the factors below.

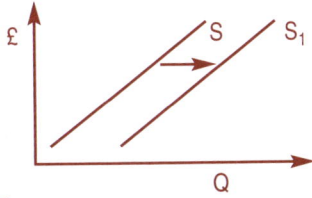

- Expectation of a future fall in price, to obtain a better price now
- A fall in the price of a **substitute in supply**
- A rise in the price of a **good in joint supply**
- Technological improvements
- Factors that reduce output directly (eg industrial disruption, natural disasters, bad weather, political disturbances

- A good that can be produced using the same resources

- Goods in joint supply are unavoidably produced together (eg hides and meat).

> The opposite effects will move the curve to the left.

The price mechanism

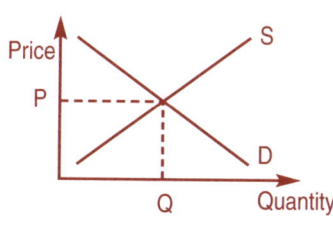

The price mechanism brings supply and demand together at the **equilibrium price** P. This is also the **market clearing price** since quantity Q is both offered and demanded and there is neither surplus nor shortage.

Functions of the price mechanism

- Market prices and their movements act as **signals** to producers, enabling them to produce what is most needed.
- When a firm operates efficiently, responding to market signals and controlling its costs, it receives a **reward** in the form of profit.
- The actions of firms in responding to the profit opportunities **allocate** resources to their best use.

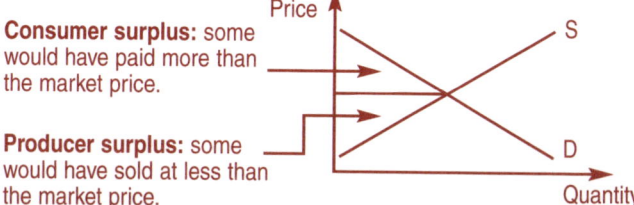

Consumer surplus: some would have paid more than the market price.

Producer surplus: some would have sold at less than the market price.

Some governments attempt to overcome market forces by **regulating prices**.

- A **maximum** price might be used to combat inflation or to make basic goods affordable.
- A **minimum** price might be used to secure the incomes of favoured producers, such as farmers.

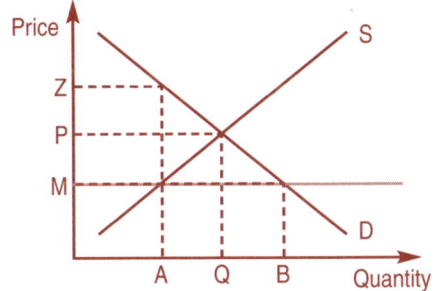

A **maximum** price set below the equilibrium price P produces a **shortage** quantity AB, since at price M, quantity B is demanded, but only quantity A is supplied. However, quantity A could be fully utilised by purchasers who are prepared to pay price Z, so a **black market** is created to divert production to these consumers at this price.

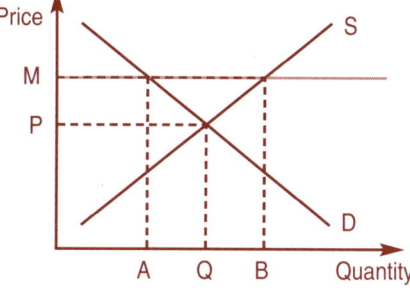

A **minimum** price set above the equilibrium price P produces a **surplus** quantity AB, since at price M, quantity A is demanded, but quantity B is supplied. Governments may introduce production **quotas**, to limit production. Alternatively, it may purchase the excess, putting it into store, or dumping it overseas, or producers might sell at less than the official minimum price.

2: The price mechanism

Notes

3: Elasticities of demand and supply

Topic List

Elasticity of demand

Elasticity of supply

Elasticity is a topic of vital importance to the important business problem of setting prices. It is also a frequent exam topic. Be sure not to overlook the various aspects of income and cross elasticity of demand.

Price elasticity of demand (PED)

A measure of the change in **demand** for a good in response to a change in its **price**: when demand is **elastic** a small change in price produces a large change in demand. When the demand is inelastic, a large change in price produces only a small change in demand.

$$PED = \frac{\text{change in quantity demanded as \% of demand}}{\text{change in price as \% of price}} = \frac{\Delta Q}{Q} \times \frac{P}{\Delta} = \frac{\Delta Q}{\Delta} \times \frac{P}{Q}$$

P and Q may be values at a **point** or averages over an **arc**.

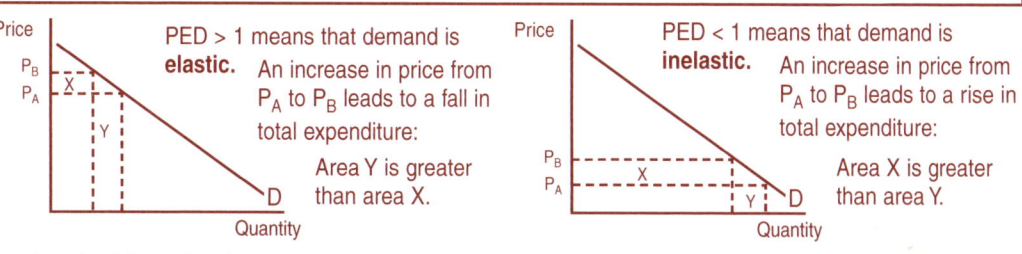

PED > 1 means that demand is **elastic.** An increase in price from P_A to P_B leads to a fall in total expenditure:

Area Y is greater than area X.

PED < 1 means that demand is **inelastic.** An increase in price from P_A to P_B leads to a rise in total expenditure:

Area X is greater than area Y.

Note that elasticity varies along a straight line demand curve!

Price | PED = 0
Demand is perfectly inelastic and remains constant at any price.
D

Price | PED = ∞
Demand is unlimited at the current price and zero at a higher price.
D

Quantity

Quantity

When PED = 1, demand responds **proportionally** to any change in price and total expenditure is constant, whatever the price.

PED is affected by

Availability of substitutes

The most important influence. Easy availability of substitutes makes demand more elastic: price rises lead to substitution.

Time horizon

Elasticity is low in the short term. Over the longer term **provision** of substitutes and awareness of them increases.

Competitors' pricing

If competitors match price changes, each one will face inelastic demand. If some increase prices and others do not, the former will face elastic demand. Unmatched price cuts have a similar effect.

Income elasticity of demand (IED)

is a measure of the change in demand for a good in response to a change **household income**. Demand for **normal goods** increases as household income rises. If demand for a good falls when household income rises, the good is an **inferior good**.

$$IED = \frac{\% \text{ change in quantity demanded}}{\% \text{ change in household income}}$$

Demand for a good is **income elastic** if its IED > 1 and **income inelastic** if IED < 1.

Cross elasticity of demand (CED)

is a measure of the change in demand for a good in response to a change in the price of another good.

$$CED = \frac{\% \text{ change in quantity of good A demanded}}{\% \text{ change in price of good B}}$$

If CED is **positive**, the goods are **substitutes** (eg a fall in the price of B will cause a fall in demand for A). If CED is **negative**, the goods are complements (eg a fall in the price of B will cause a rise in demand for A).

A change in household income or the price of another good shifts the demand curve to the left or right

The **elasticity of supply** of a good indicates the responsiveness of supply to the change in price. It is a measure of firms' ability to adjust the quantity of goods they supply.

$$\text{Elasticity of supply} = \frac{\% \text{ change in quantity supplied}}{\% \text{ change in price}}$$

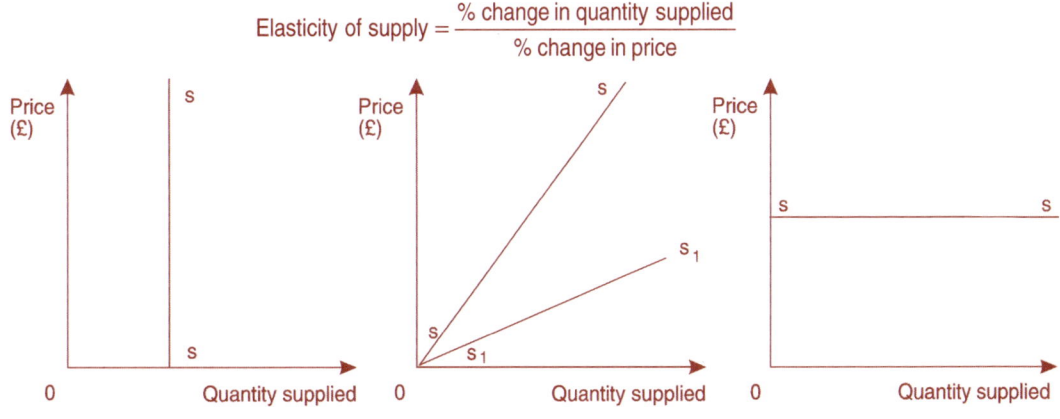

3: Elasticities of demand and supply

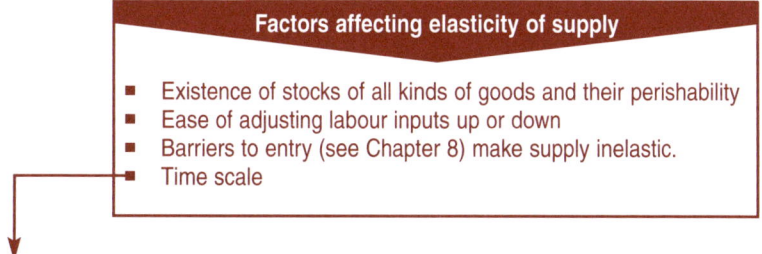

Factors affecting elasticity of supply

- Existence of stocks of all kinds of goods and their perishability
- Ease of adjusting labour inputs up or down
- Barriers to entry (see Chapter 8) make supply inelastic.
- Time scale

Elasticities vary with time

- During the **market period** only existing stocks and levels of output are available. Supply is **very inelastic**.
- Over the **short run**, quantities can be adjusted by working overtime or short time. Supply is **quite elastic**.
- Over the **long run** plant can be built or shut down. Supply is **very elastic**.

3: Elasticities of demand and supply

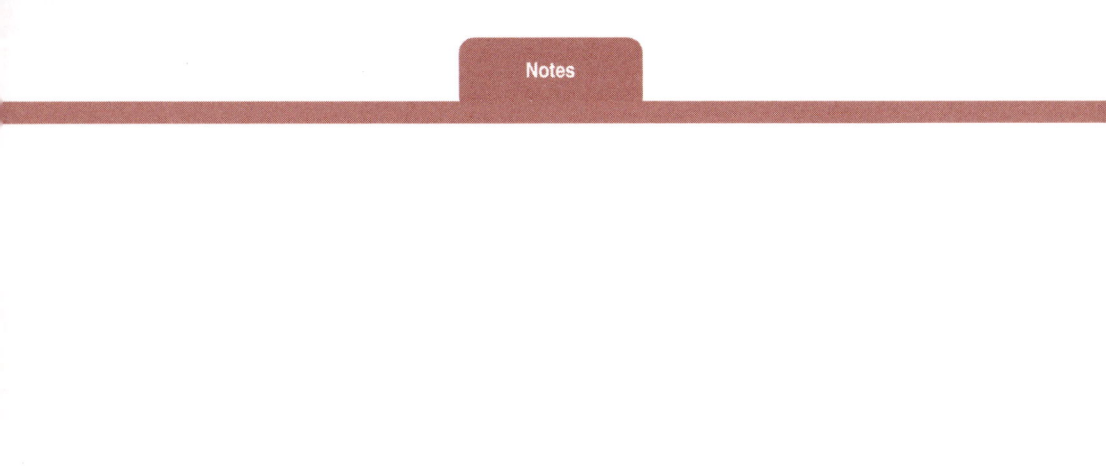

Notes

Topic List

Market imperfection

Costs and benefits

Indirect taxes and subsidies

Market failure occurs when the market mechanism fails to produce the most efficient allocation of resources. This occurs when there are market imperfections and when private costs and social costs differ. The need to consider non-market goals and to provide public goods and merit goods are also difficult to satisfy with purely market-based solutions.

Market imperfections

Imperfect knowledge

Market efficiency is dependent on all parties having complete information about which goods are available and at which prices. When this knowledge is not widely available, prices and hence resource allocation will tend to remain fixed.

Time is needed for the market mechanism to have effect. This slows down changes in resource allocation.

Monopoly elements

(Monopoly is covered in more detail in Chapter 8.) If a firm controls all or much of the supply of a good it can restrict output and thus drive up price.

Similarly, a **monopsonist** purchaser can exact concessions on price from suppliers.

Factors of production can also be subject to monopolistic practices.

Scarce resources → Private costs → Supplier ← Profit ← **AN ECONOMIC TRANSACTION** → Private benefits → Purchaser

Social costs   −ve EXTERNALITIES +ve   Social benefits

Social costs and benefits may differ from private cost and benefits.

Public goods

- Consumption by one individual or group does not significantly reduce availability.
- It is difficult or impossible to control access to the good. Thus, there is no incentive to pay for it: people can be **free riders.**
- Examples are lighthouses and national security.

Merit goods (and demerit goods)

- Society places a different value on these goods from the value placed on them by the individual.
- Merit goods have positive externalities (eg education), demerit goods have negative externalities (eg smoking).
- It is a widely accepted role of government to promote consumption of merit goods and to reduce consumption of demerit goods.

Indirect taxes and subsidies can be used to align private costs and benefits with social costs and benefits.

Indirect taxes can be used to increase private costs to reflect negative externalities, such as the emission of pollutants, while subsidies can be used to promote the consumption of merit goods. Subsidies are also used to protect politically favoured industries.

Effect of a direct tax

- Price paid by the consumer → P_1
- Equilibrium price before imposition of tax → P_0
- Price retained by the supplier after paying over tax receipts to government → P_2

- Indirect tax is collected from the supplier, so has effect as an extra cost. Supply curve shifts upwards.
- Supply curve before tax is imposed
- Initial equilibrium point

Areas A and B represent the extent of the tax burden on the purchaser and suppliers respectively.

The elasticities of both demand and supply affect the relative sizes of areas A and B.

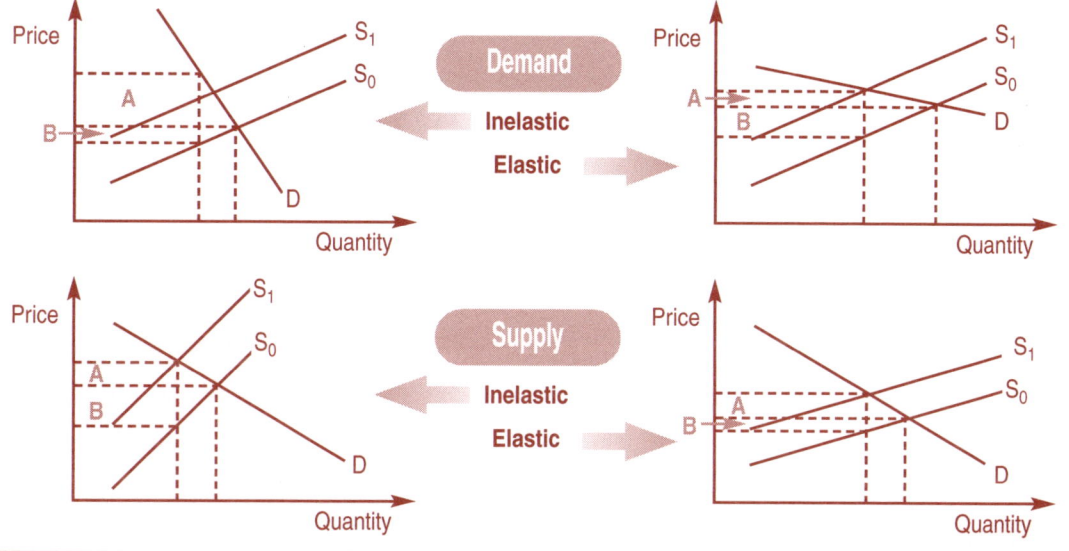

A **subsidy** works like an indirect tax in reverse.

Price to the consumer falls from P_0 to P_1, which is less than the total value of the subsidy.

The supplier benefits by the amount $P_1 - P_2$.

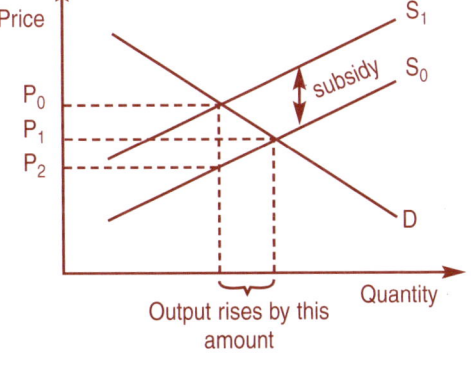

Subsidy is paid to the supplier to cover some cost - supply curve shifts downwards.

The relative benefit to supplier and consumers depends on the elasticities of supply and demand.

5: Production and costs

Topic List

This chapter contains some diagrams of fundamental importance for your examination success. Your understanding will be enhanced if you are able to draw them and explain what they mean.

The **short run** is the period of time during which the amount of at least one factor of production is fixed.

The **long run** allows all factors of production to be adjusted in quantity.

Factor of production	Its cost
Land	Rent
Labour	Wages
Capital	Interest
Enterprise	Profit

A firm's short run costs

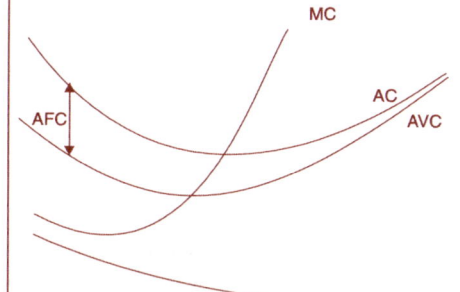

- **Total cost** is made up of fixed costs and variable costs.
- **Average cost** is made up of average fixed cost per unit and average variable cost per unit.
- **Marginal cost** is the addition to total cost caused by producing one more unit.
- **Normal profit** is a cost of production.
- Variable cost and marginal cost are not the same thing.
- The marginal cost curve always crosses the average cost curve at its lowest point. Beyond this point it represents the firm's **supply curve**.

The short run average cost curve is U shaped

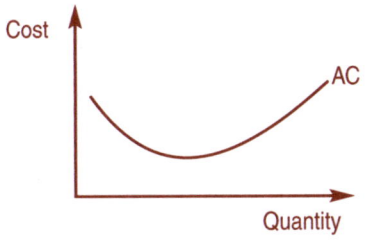

Cost

AC

Quantity

It **falls initially** for 2 reasons.

- **Specialisation** or the division of labour. Specialisation enhances efficiency since staff become more proficient at their specialised tasks

- **Utilisation of indivisibilities.** When plant is not operated at full capacity its costs must be spread over fewer output units. Average cost falls as output approaches capacity.

Eventually the curve begins to rise. The law of **diminishing returns** tells us that if one or more factors of production are fixed in quantity but the input of another is variable, the extra output generated by each extra unit of input will eventually begin to fall. This is because the extra input has less and less of the fixed factor(s) to work with.

Total revenue (TR): total proceeds of selling a given quantity of output

Average revenue (AR): price per unit

Marginal revenue (MR): the addition to total revenue from the sale of one extra unit

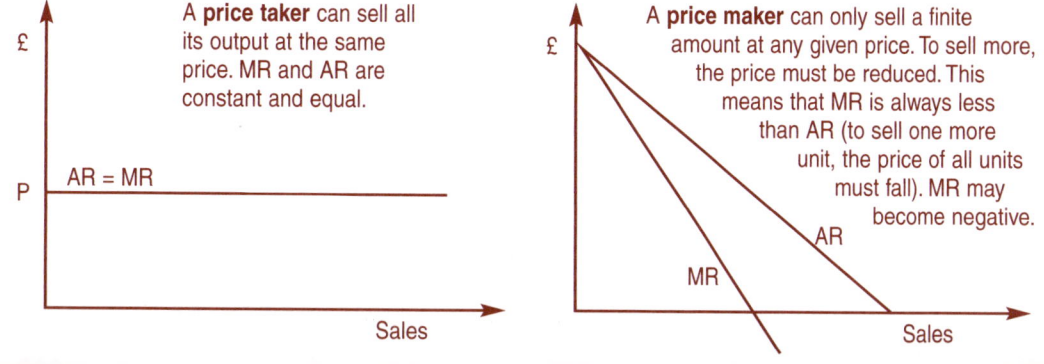

A **price taker** can sell all its output at the same price. MR and AR are constant and equal.

AR = MR

A **price maker** can only sell a finite amount at any given price. To sell more, the price must be reduced. This means that MR is always less than AR (to sell one more unit, the price of all units must fall). MR may become negative.

Profits are maximised at the level of output where MC = MR

Profit maximisation for a price maker

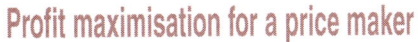

At outputs less than P_{max} the extra cost of making an extra unit is less than the extra revenue from selling it.

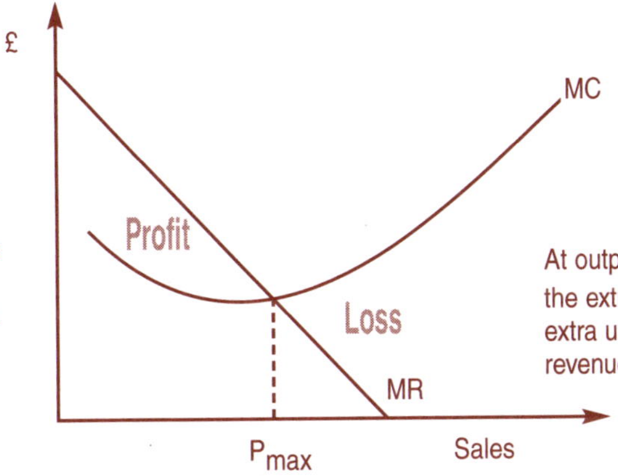

£
MC
Profit
Loss
MR
Pmax
Sales

At outputs greater than P_{max} the extra cost of making an extra unit exceeds the revenue from selling it.

In the long run it is possible to expand production by increasing the quantity of all factors of production employed. In many cases, though not all, **economies of scale** cause the whole cost structure to move downwards. **Diseconomies of scale** may eventually arise, producing a **U shaped long run average cost curve (LRAC).**

Cost (£)

SRAC₁
SRAC₂
SRAC₃
SRAC₄ SRAC₅ SRAC₆
LRAC

Economies of scale

Constant returns to scale

Diseconomies of scale

Minimum efficient scale

Output

Diseconomies of scale largely relate to human factors such as management effectiveness and problems of communications and culture.

Internal ← **Economies of scale** → External

- Technical: Dimensional economies; indivisibilities
- Commercial: bulk purchasing; stockholding
- Financial: increased creditworthiness

(due to growth of industry)
- Skilled labour pool
- Specialised suppliers
- Dedicated infrastructure

5: Production and costs

Notes

6: Factor markets

Topic List

Derived demand

Capital and interest

Labour and wages

Land and rent

Factor markets are included in the CIMA syllabus, but the Examiner appears not to regard them as particularly important, apart from investment and the market for capital.

Firms' demand for factors of production is derived from households' demand for the goods and services the firms produce.

The demand for the factors of production thus depends on the demand for the goods and services they are used to produce rather than the inherent nature of the factors themselves.

Factor rewards

Land is rewarded with **rent.**

Labour is rewarded with **wages**.

Capital is rewarded with **interest**.

determined by supply and demand

Enterprise is rewarded with **profit**. **Normal profit** is earned when total revenues equal the total opportunity costs of all input resources, including enterprise, and is sufficient to persuade the entrepreneur not to transfer the resources to another type of business.

The marginal efficiency of capital (MEC)

Firms will commit capital to a project if it is profitable, ie if its IRR (see Business Mathematics Passcards) is greater than the interest payable on the capital. The higher the rate of interest payable, the fewer the feasible projects.

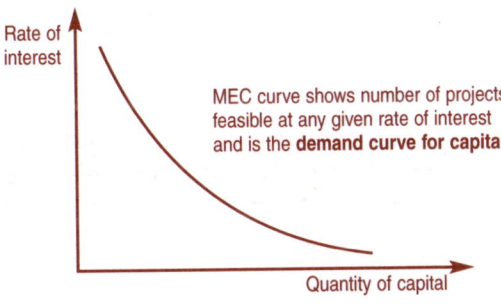

MEC curve shows number of projects feasible at any given rate of interest and is the **demand curve for capital**.

The supply of capital

Capital is supplied by the savings of households and the quantity available depends to some extent on the rate of interest payable: a higher rate makes savings more attractive. However, the number of viable projects falls as interest rates rise, so the level of investment depends on the normal operation of market forces of supply and demand. The picture is further complicated by the fact that interest rates are influenced by the Central Bank's base rate.

The **marginal revenue product** (MRP) of labour is the extra revenue a firm can obtain from selling the output of one more worker. The MRP curve slopes downwards because of diminishing returns. It is the demand curve for labour. Each type of labour has its own MRP curve, since the output of some types of labour is more valuable than that of other types. Firms generally will expand output until the MRP equals the marginal cost of labour.

Wage rate £

MRP of CIMA member

MRP of less valued member

Number employed

Wage rates and labour supply

- **Substitution effect:** a wage rise increases the opportunity cost of leisure. Workers may substitute work for leisure. **Supply of labour increases.**
- **Income effect:** higher income may lead to higher consumption of all kinds including 'consumption' of leisure. **Supply of labour falls.**

Causes of labour immobility

- Professional entry barriers
- Ignorance of remote opportunities
- Differential housing costs
- Non-monetary factors, eg suitability of schooling
- Linguistic and cultural barriers
- Discrimination
- Ability requirements

The effect of a minimum wage

All other things being equal, a minimum wage set above the market clearing price is likely to lead to excess supply in the form of unemployment (see Chapter 2).

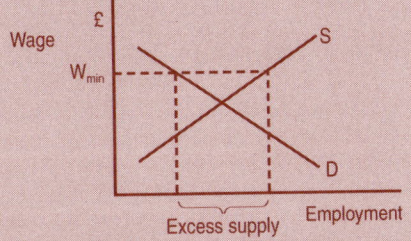

However, when **monopsonist purchasers** of low grade labour hold wages down, they are likely to have **vacancies**. A minimum wage will lead to those vacancies being filled.

The elasticity of demand for labour
Principal factors

- Technical ease of substituting other factors of production

- Elasticity of supply of other factors of production

- Elasticity of demand for the final product

- Proportion of labour costs to total costs: a low proportion of labour costs leads to inelastic demand and vice versa

The total amount of land available may be regarded as fixed. Under these circumstances, in the primary sector, rent will be determined by the goods produced from the land. Where land can be used for more than one purpose (agriculture or building, say) an upward sloping supply curve will exist and rent will be determined by its interaction with the downward sloping marginal revenue product curve (demand curve).

Transfer earnings and economic rent

Transfer earnings are the opportunity cost of a factor of production. Any excess of actual reward over transfer earnings are **economic rent**. Do not confuse transfer earnings with **transfer payments** (see Chapter 13). **Economic rent** is conceptually very similar to **producer surplus** (see Chapter 2) but applies to factors of production rather than goods.

7: Organisations in a mixed economy

Topic List

Sectors of the economy

Objectives of firms

Growth of firms

Industry location decisions

This chapter covers three related topics to do with the way economic activity is organised.

Two approaches to analysing the economy

Public sector

Activities undertaken by government including defence, justice, security, health and education; and businesses owned by government, ie nationalised industries.

Private sector

Includes not-for-profit organisations such as charities and profit making businesses. Sole traders and partners have **unlimited liability**. Shareholders in companies or corporations do not. Incorporated businesses may be divided into those that may offer shares to the public (UK plc) and those that may not (UK Ltd).

Primary sector Produces raw materials: agriculture, forestry, mining, oil and gas production

Secondary sector Manufacture of goods; construction; energy; water

Tertiary sector Provides services, including distribution, catering and public services

As they grow, national economies tend to develop from having a dominant primary sector to having a much more important secondary sector and eventually to consisting largely of the tertiary sector.

Basic economic theory assumes that firms operate so as to maximise profit for their owners.

The **separation of ownership from control** in larger companies has led to other suggestions, since managers are likely to promote their own personal ambitions for pay, power and status.

Managerial models of the firm

Baumol: sales maximisation

Managers benefit from expanding sales, with prestige, bonuses and security. The company benefits since the increased market share brings economies of scale.

Williamson: management discretion

Managers act to maximise their own rewards subject to a minimum profit requirement.

Cyert and March: organisational coalition

Political compromise is necessary between the various interested groups, or **stakeholders**: managers, shareholders, employees and customers.

7: Organisations in a mixed economy

Two routes to growth

→ **Organic growth** of the firm's own resources via increased sales and gradual expansion.

→ **Growth through mergers and takeovers** by joining existing firms together.

Vertical integration links firms with their suppliers (backward) or customers (forward integration). This gives control over markets and sources of supply but brings few economies of scale and creates considerable problems for management.

Horizontal integration links firms doing the same sort of business with the same kind of customers and suppliers. It brings economies of scale and market power but may attract anti-monopoly attention.

Conglomerate diversification merges quite unrelated businesses. This spreads risk of failure and can be counter-cyclical.

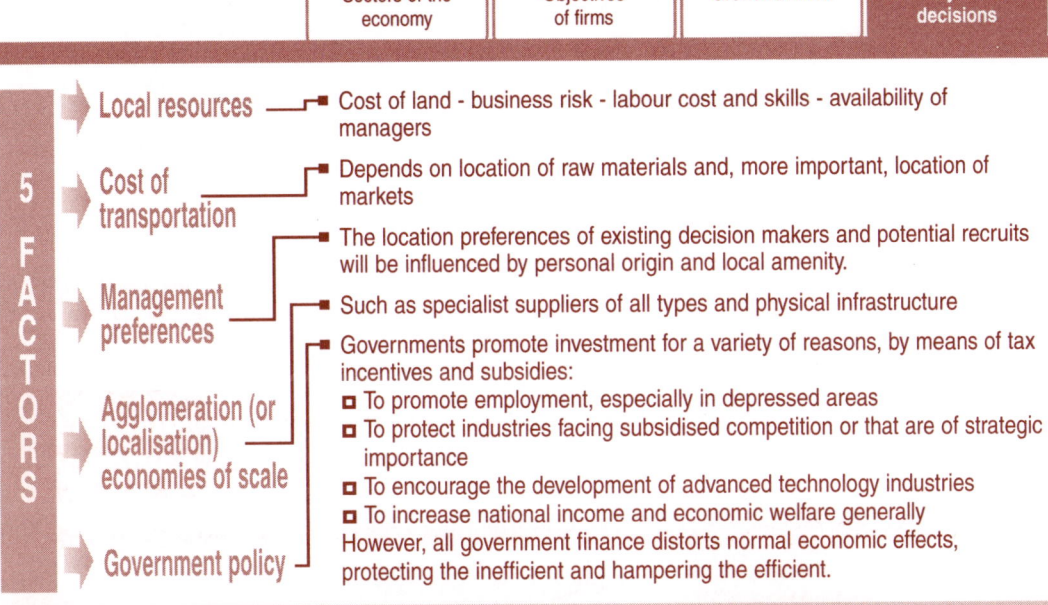

5 FACTORS

Local resources — Cost of land - business risk - labour cost and skills - availability of managers

Cost of transportation — Depends on location of raw materials and, more important, location of markets

Management preferences — The location preferences of existing decision makers and potential recruits will be influenced by personal origin and local amenity.

Such as specialist suppliers of all types and physical infrastructure

Agglomeration (or localisation) economies of scale — Governments promote investment for a variety of reasons, by means of tax incentives and subsidies:
- To promote employment, especially in depressed areas
- To protect industries facing subsidised competition or that are of strategic importance
- To encourage the development of advanced technology industries
- To increase national income and economic welfare generally

However, all government finance distorts normal economic effects, protecting the inefficient and hampering the efficient.

Government policy

Notes

*The perfectly competitive firm displays **technical efficiency**: it produces where AC is minimised; and **allocative efficiency**: the market uses factors of production in the correct quantity to supply as much as is demanded at the market price.*

Perfect competition and monopoly are two extremes. Between them they illustrate most of the important ideas concerning markets, so they are fundamental. They are not, however, often found in the real world.

The perfectly competitive market

- There are many buyers and sellers; each firm is price taker, unable to influence market price
- Buyers and sellers act rationally and have the same information

- The product is homogeneous
- There is free entry and exit for firms
- There are no transport or information costs

In the short run the number of firms is fixed. Firms many make losses or supernormal profits by operating at the profit maximising level of output, ie where MC = MR.

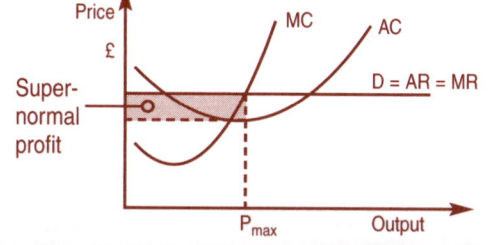

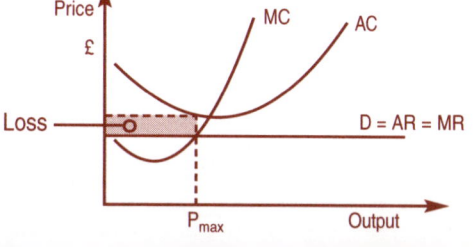

In the **long run**, super-normal profit is competed away and loss-making firms leave the industry. The remaining firms can only make normal profit and will operate where MC = MR = AC = AR = price per unit.

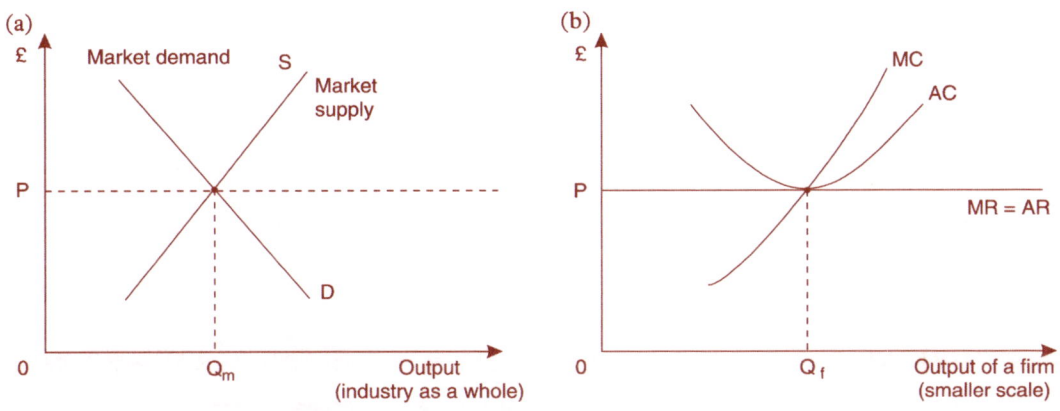

(a)

£

Market demand

S

Market supply

P

0   Q$_m$ Output (industry as a whole)

D

(b)

£

MC

AC

P

MR = AR

0   Q$_f$ Output of a firm (smaller scale)

By restricting output to Q, the monopolist can charge a price greater than average cost; it thus makes supernormal profit XYZP. This represents **consumer surplus** transferred to the monopolist. The area WYZ is consumer surplus totally lost and is called the **deadweight loss** of monopoly.

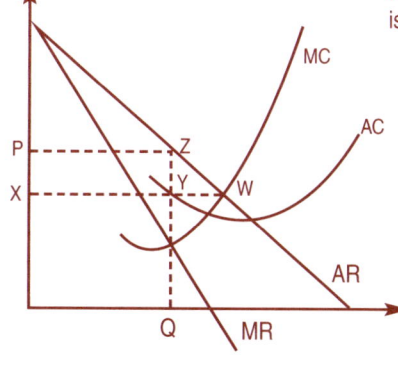

For a monopolist, the firm's AR curve is the market demand curve.

The monopolist has market power and can increase sales by reducing price. As a result AR falls as output increases and MR is always less than AR. MR becomes negative when demand becomes inelastic and further price cuts, though increasing volume, reduce turnover.

The monopolist restricts output to Q in order to maximise profit by producing where MC = MR.

Q is not at the lowest point on the AC curve: the monopolist produces less than under perfect competition and at a higher cost. **Monopoly does not display allocative or technical efficiency.**

Barriers to entry

Barriers to entry prevent other firms from challenging the monopolist's privileged position.

Barriers to entry

- **Legal** (eg nationalisation law and patents)
- **Absolute cost** (eg privileged access to cheap raw materials)
- **High fixed costs** regardless of market share (eg creating the infrastructure for a phone network)
- **Economies of scale** where the long run average cost curve falls indefinitely and new entrants do not have sufficient market share to operate cheaply
- **Product differentiation:** an existing product with a powerful brand can create customer loyalty, thus imposing very high promotion costs on a new entrant

Price discrimination

occurs when a firm sells the same product at different prices in different markets.

- The seller must be able to control the supply of the product. Clearly a monopolist can.
- The seller must be able to prevent the resale of the product. Grouping by status (eg age), time, geography, permits this. Customer ignorance helps the supplier.
- Elasticity of demand must vary between the markets, so that some customers are wiling to pay a higher price.

X inefficiency

As well as technical and allocative inefficiency, monopolies display X inefficiency: they have little incentive to control costs so their AC curve moves upwards.

For monopoly

- If LRAC falls indefinitely as output increases, and **economies of scale** continue to rise, the monopolist can charge lower prices than perfect competition. This is evident in a **natural monopoly**.
- Monopolies can spend more on R&D.
- Monopolies find it easier to raise capital for new ventures, which aids economic growth.
- Supernormal profits stimulate competition; a temporary monopoly under a patent may encourage further improvements.
- Patent rights reward innovation and entrepreneurial flair, both of which are needed for continuing economic growth.

Against monopoly

- The monopolist's supernormal profit is obtained at the expense of the consumer.
- Monopolies display technical, allocative and X inefficiency.
- Monopolists resort to restrictive practices such as price discrimination to further increase their profits.
- **Product differentiation** wastes resources in the pursuit of monopoly advantages.
- **Diseconomies of scale** may arise.
- If a monopolist controls a vital resource, it can take decisions that affect the **public interest adversely**.

Topic List

Monopolistic competition

Oligopoly

*This chapter deals with the two other important theoretical market models and includes a note about **contestable markets**. Make sure that you understand the difference between monopoly and monopolistic competition.*

Monopolistic competition differs from perfect competition in that firm's products are comparable rather than homogeneous.

Firms try to achieve monopoly profits by **product differentiation**. This gives each firm power over its own market price. They are thus **price-makers** and experience downward sloping demand/AR and MR curves.

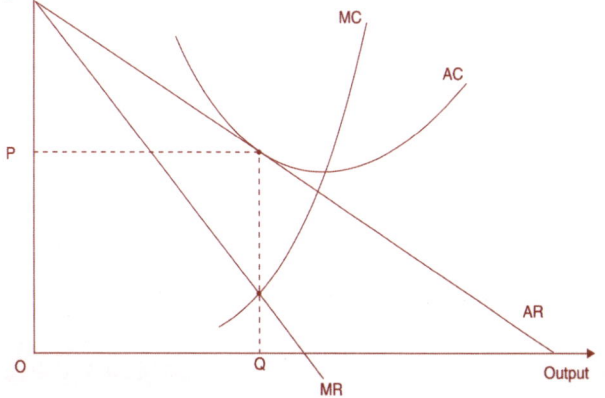

Features of monopolistic competition

- In the **short run** the firm can make supernormal profits by shifting the demand/AR curve to the right. The diagram is then exactly like that of the monopolist in the long run (see Chapter 8).
- Because there is no real barriers to entry, these profits can probably be competed away; the demand curve shifts back left to produce the long run equilibrium shown in the diagram.
- Like monopoly, monopolistic competition does not produce where AC is at a minimum; it is technically inefficient.
- The firm will probably always have **excess capacity**, for the same reason.
- The extent to which the product differentiation is real and thus a source of utility or spuriously created by advertising will vary from time to time and product to product.

A **contestable market** is similar to perfect competition, though there are few suppliers. A lack of entry and exit barriers deters firms from trying to obtain supernormal profit. The firm produces at minimum AC and where AC = MC = MR = AR, just as in perfect competition.

In an oligopoly there are a few large suppliers. These suppliers are interdependent in their decision making: they must consider their competitor's responses to any changes they make.

The kinked oligopoly demand curve illustrates the interdependent decision making of competing oligopolies. While the oligopolist has market power, any change in price is likely to be met with a powerful response.

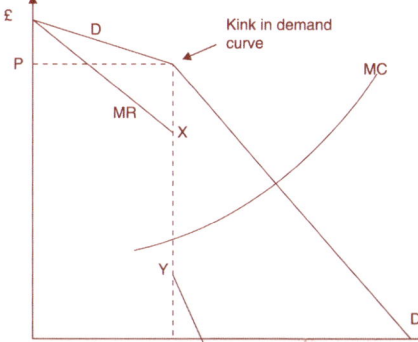

- The demand is **elastic** at levels above P since a price rise by one firm would not be matched and purchasers would deal with other suppliers.

- The demand curve is **inelastic** below P: competitors would match any price cut by one firm and so market share would not change very much.

Oligopolists may not compete at all. There may be an informally acknowledged price leader who sets the prevailing price or there may be a formal cartel agreement to control price by restricting output. This is illegal in the US and EU, though some countries have official schemes for favoured industries.

Notes

10: Public policy and competition

Topic List

Government control

Promoting competition

There are many aspects to the theme covered in this chapter, many of them as much political as economic.

Governments intervene in microeconomic matters when market forces do not produce the outcomes they wish to see. The various aspects of **market failure** invite government regulation. The extreme form of intervention is **nationalisation** and this may be undertaken for other reasons.

Government response to market failure

- **Monopoly elements** – controls on prices or profits - breaking up monopoly companies ('trust busting')

- **Externalities** – regulations (eg to control pollution, compel car insurance, ban smoking)

- **Imperfect information** – product safety rules, public service advertising, provision of jobcentres

Other justifications for nationalisation

- **Natural monopolies** should not be allowed to exploit their position (eg utilities companies)
- Larger groupings could exploit further economies of scale to natural advantage (eg aerospace)
- Only government can supply enough finance for some industries (eg railway networks)
- Political control over strategic industries (eg oil production)
- Marxist/socialist theory. The political left is more or less uncomfortable with capitalism and wishes to control industry for the benefit of its client groups (eg coal mining)

There has been a move away from government control of industry in the West over the last 20 years.

Reasons for reducing the degree of government control

- Nationalised industries being run for the convenience of their staffs rather than their customers
- Civil servants and politicians not good at commercial decision making
- Sale of state assets permits tax cuts and reduces need for government borrowing
- Enhanced competition seen as likely to improve efficiency and promote growth
- Reduction in enforcement costs and unintended consequences of regulation
- Wider share ownership

Privatisation

It is possible to discern several strands in privatisation.

- **Deregulation**, to allow private firms to compete with state-owned ones (eg postal services)
- **Contracting out** of government work previously done by government employees (eg waste collection)
- **Outright sale** of businesses to private shareholders (eg British Telecom)

Privatisation has been criticised

- Creation of private monopolies
- Sale of assets at a discount
- Enhanced top executive benefits
- Decline in quantity and quality of service

Western governments promote competition in most areas of economic activity since it is a simple and cheap way to achieve economic efficiency and growth.

The UK Competition Commission

The CC may investigate when one firm controls 25% of the market or when a merger involves more than £75m of assets worldwide. It reports to the government. It seeks to promote consumer interests, competition, enterprise and efficiency and tries to balance rewards for innovation and the benefits of scale economies against the disadvantages of monopoly.

11: The monetary environment

Topic List

Money

Financial intermediation

Interest rates

The various aspects of the monetary environment are a fruitful source of MCQs though most concern various aspects of monetary policy, which is dealt with in Chapters 15 and 16. They are also important for understanding government policy. You must understand the nature and functions of money and the impact of inflation.

Commodity money and token money

Units of commodity money have intrinsic value (eg gold, cowrie shells, cigarettes). Token money (eg bank notes, certificates of deposit) can be provided in much greater quantities and makes the valuable resources useable in production.

Inflation

Inflation is an erosion of the purchasing power of money over time. Its causes are dealt with in Chapter 15. Inflation changes the value of money and hence affects its ability to perform its functions.

Functions of money	Effects of inflation
1 **Means of exchange:** enables trade to take place without barter, enhancing speed and scope (the other functions flow from this).	Very high inflation can lead to flight from money to a more stable substitute such as foreign currency or commodity money, or a system of barter.
2 **Unit of account:** different goods can be valued for different purposes of trade.	The values of goods do not all decline by the same amount under inflation.
3 **Standard of deferred payment:** definition of value over time permits offering of credit.	Creditors lose value and debtors' liabilities are effectively reduced.
4 **Liquid store of value:** can be converted into other assets without delay or loss of value.	Money retains its **nominal** value but loses its **real** value. Money assets are likely to be converted into a more tangible form.

The amount of money in an economy is called the **money stock** or **money supply** and is measured in terms of **monetary aggregates**.

The money supply must rise to accommodate economic growth. Too fast a rise in the money supply indicates that inflation is taking place.

Narrow money

is a measure of the money that is immediately available for current spending.

Broad money

is a measure of the money that is easily available for spending. It includes narrow money and money held in the form of savings that could be obtained without capital loss.

UK monetary aggregates

M0 consists principally of notes and coin in circulation outside the Bank of England. It also includes banks' operational deposits with the Bank of England.

M4 includes private sector notes and coin, interest bearing deposits with banks and building societies, building society share accounts and other interest bearing deposits. It is about 25-30 times larger than M0.

Financial intermediaries provide the facilities and **financial instruments** to transfer funds from **surplus units**, or lenders, to **deficit units** or borrowers in the business, personal, overseas and government sectors.

Financial intermediaries

- **Clearing** or **retail banks** provide banking services to the public.

- **Merchant banks** provide advice and major finance to corporate clients.

- **Discount houses** provide short term loan finance to institutions.

- Insurance companies, pension funds, unit trusts and investment trusts make longer term investments primarily for private clients.

Functions of financial intermediaries

- **Aggregation:** relatively small deposits can be combined into major loans for borrowers
- **Maturity transformation:** by receiving a constant flow of deposits, interest and repayments, depositors' desire for liquidity can be satisfied at the same time as borrowers are provided with long term funds
- **Security:** a, financially sound, intermediary can absorb bad debts and guarantee depositors' funds
- **Convenience for lenders:** lenders are relieved of the need for find their own credit worthy borrowers.
- **Source of funds:** similarly, borrowers are assisted to obtain the funds they need

Nominal and real rates of interest

- **Nominal rates** of interest are expressed in terms of money return

- Real rates of interest are adjusted for the changing value of money

$$\frac{1 + \text{money rate}}{1 + \text{inflation rate}} = 1 + \text{real rate}$$

The term structure of interest rates

This normal yield curve illustrates the way interest rates vary with the term of the loan. There is greater risk of losses from default and inflation the longer the term of the loan. Longer term loans therefore attract higher rates.

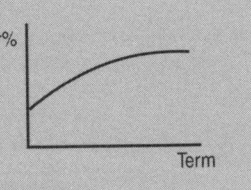

Interest rates are also influenced by other factors that contribute to **risk**. These include the perceived **credit worthiness** of the borrower and whether the loan is secured by a **charge** over property.

11: The monetary environment

Notes

12: Financial institutions

Topic List

Banking and credit creation

The central bank

Financial markets

Sources of finance

Banks' ability to create money in the form of credit is something you must understand thoroughly since it is fundamental to much government macroeconomic management. The various details of the financial markets and sources of finance are a potential source of MCQs.

Functions of the UK commercial banks

- **Payments mechanism:** payments made by cheque are **cleared** and net balances transferred via banks' deposits at the Bank of England

- **Storage and safeguarding of wealth:** most accounts attract interest

- **Lending money:** banks earn income by charging interest on term loans and overdrafts. See credit creation below

- **Financial intermediation:** see above

- **Business services:** foreign exchange dealing; bill discounting; business advice; insurance broking; provision of letters of credit; factoring debts and so on

Banks and assets and liabilities

Banks aim to use money in their possession to make **profits**. At the same time they have to ensure the **security** of their assets and maintain sufficient **liquidity** to meet their customers' requirements for cash. They therefore maintain an asset structure of graduated liquidity and profitability.

More liquid ↕ More profitable

Cash
Market loans (money at call and short notice)
Bills (usually repayable in 90 days)
Advances (term loans)
Investments

Central banks use the **Basle Agreement** rules on **capital adequacy** to supervise their banks and ensure they have sufficient provision for bad debts.

The **bank** or **credit multiplier** is the name given to banks' ability to **create credit**, and hence money, by maintaining their cash reserves at less than 100% of the value of the deposits they hold.

The basics of credit creation

We saw in Chapter 11 that the total amount of money in the UK economy is many times the amount of cash in circulation. Even when cheque transactions are taken into account, most money is on deposit at any given time. This means that a bank receiving a deposit is able to lend most of it out, retaining only a small proportion to meet the depositor's needs. The money lent is in turn deposited and supports a further loan.

The credit multiplier

The relationship between the amount of a deposit and the credit that can be based on it is called the credit multiplier and takes the form:

$$\text{Deposits} = \frac{\text{Cash}}{\text{Cash ratio}}$$

Where the cash ratio is the percentage of the cash deposited the bank feels it prudent **not** to lend. Thus with a cash ratio of 20%, a cash receipt of £1,000 can support total deposits of £5,000: the £1,000 originally paid in and £4,000 credited to borrowers accounts.

12: Financial institutions

A country's central bank plays a vital role in the management of the monetary system. The functions of any given central bank may vary from those of another, especially in the areas of monetary policy and financial supervision. The Bank of England is, since 1998, a good example of modern trends.

Functions of the Bank of England

- Provides banking services to the government
- Central note issuing authority
- Manages the National Debt
- Banker to the commercial banks, holding operational deposits to permit interbank transfers; can require special deposits to control money supply; lender of last resort
- Manages national foreign currency reserves
- Monetary Policy Committee sets the UK's interest rates

Setting interest rates

Since 1998 the Bank has been responsible for setting the UK's interest rates in order to achieve the government's inflation target of 2.5%. Central bank independent control over interest rates is now widely accepted as an effective control over inflation. Conversely, the Bank's interest rate policy must also take account of the need to expand the money supply to support economic growth.

The Bank no longer supervises the banking system. This role has been transferred to the Financial Services Authority.

Capital markets

- The **London Stock Exchange** provides, regulates and supervises a number of markets for securities.

    ① **Equities** market for the **issue** of new equities, options and convertible securities and **trading** of existing issues

    ② **Alternative Investment Market** for smaller companies' securities

    ③ **Gilt edged market** for UK government stock

- **International capital markets** are operated between banks in larger countries to provide major finance for very large companies and institutions. Confusingly, their securities are known as Eurobonds.

In the US, public stock issues that are not traded on any domestic stock exchange are traded in the **over the counter** market, largely via the NASDAQ system.

Money markets

Short term investment and borrowing of funds is handled in the **money markets**. These are operated by the banks and other financial institutions and include markets for:

- Certificates of deposit
- Bills of exchange and commercial paper
- Treasury bills
- Building society bulk borrowing
- Local authority bills and other short term borrowing

12: Financial institutions

Sources of finance for companies

- Issue of **share capital**: complex, with considerations relating to control, existing rights, authorised share capital and company status - Ltd or plc.

- **Borrowing**: more flexible, but likely to require **security**. Capital **gearing** may also be an issue.

- **Retained profits**: none of the complications of the methods above, but may not be available in cash form.

Venture capital in the UK is normally sourced from 3i, a consortium of UK banks, and can take the form of both debt and equity. The main users of venture capital have been start-ups and management buy-outs. Many venture capital projects end in failure so the providers of capital require a high return and a clear exit route.

Notes

13: National income and its measurement

Topic List

National income

Circular flow

Measuring national income

This chapter introduces the important idea of national income and the mechanism of the circular flow. All macroeconomic ideas refer to these basic ideas, so the material in this chapter and the next are a fruitful source of questions.

A country's national income is the value of the economic wealth its people create in a year by undertaking economic activity, that is, by providing goods and services.

The measurement national income is subject to conventions and errors of measurement

- Work done by people for themselves is not included, nor is barter trade
- The size of the undeclared or 'black' economy is, by definition, unknown
- Government services are included at cost; commercially provided services valuation includes an element of profit

Why calculate national income?

- Assist government economic planning
- Permit international comparison
- Measure standard of living

Standard of living is normally expressed in terms of national income per head of population. This is useful for establishing trends but must be used with care for international comparisons.

The national income a country generates does not necessarily achieve its potential level: the economy may be operating inefficiently, to the left of its production possibility curve (see Chapter 1). This would imply that some scarce resources were being under utilised.

The circular flow of income in the economy has a real existence which is reflected by money flows.

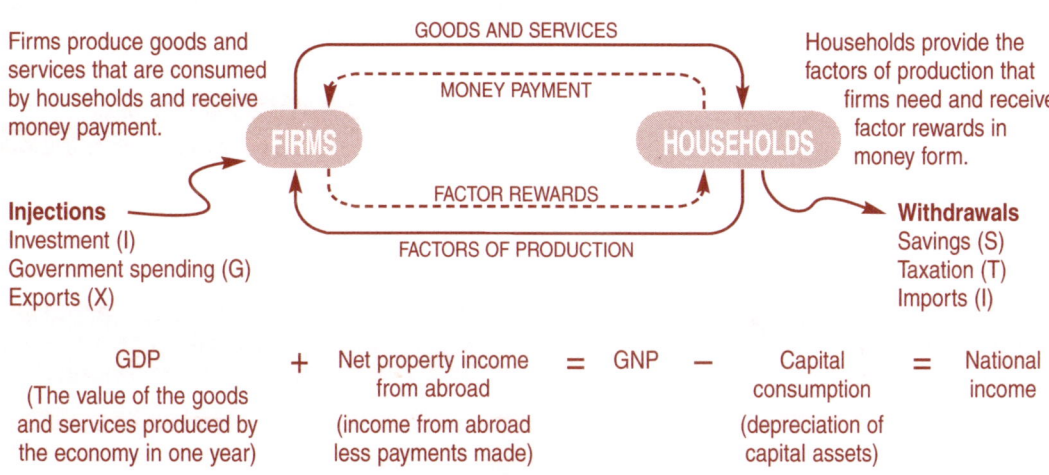

Firms produce goods and services that are consumed by households and receive money payment.

FIRMS

GOODS AND SERVICES

MONEY PAYMENT

FACTOR REWARDS

FACTORS OF PRODUCTION

HOUSEHOLDS

Households provide the factors of production that firms need and receive factor rewards in money form.

Injections
Investment (I)
Government spending (G)
Exports (X)

Withdrawals
Savings (S)
Taxation (T)
Imports (I)

GDP + Net property income from abroad = GNP − Capital consumption = National income

(The value of the goods and services produced by the economy in one year)

(income from abroad less payments made)

(depreciation of capital assets)

Expenditure approach

Expenditure by consumers and government is added to the value of exports. Firm's purchases of goods and services other than capital goods and year-end stocks are excluded to avoid double counting. Indirect taxes and the value of imports must then be deducted.

This approach is considered the most reliable.

Income approach

Before tax income from employment and self employment, employer's payroll taxes (National Insurance in the UK) and firms' gross profits are added to rent from property and any trading surplus from government owned enterprise. From this must be deducted an allowance for appreciation of stocks and a charge for capital consumption.

Note that government pensions and welfare benefits are **transfer payments** and are not included.

Value-added approach

Since the provision of goods and services involves firms taking inputs of the factors of production plus materials and components, a measure of **total** output can be obtained by totalling the value added by firms. Value added is defined as the sales value of the firm's output less the cost of goods and services bought in from other firms. (The cost of factors of production is **not** deducted.)

14: The determination of national income

The chapter starts our coverage of this important topic.

General level of prices

AS

AD

National income

In the simplest terms, the macroeconomy is the aggregate of all the nation's individual markets for goods and services. Aggregate supply and aggregate demand curves intersect to determine the overall level of output (national income) and the general level of prices.

However, the equilibrium is **not stable**. Cyclical changes in the level of output (the trade cycle) and changes in the value of money complicate the picture.

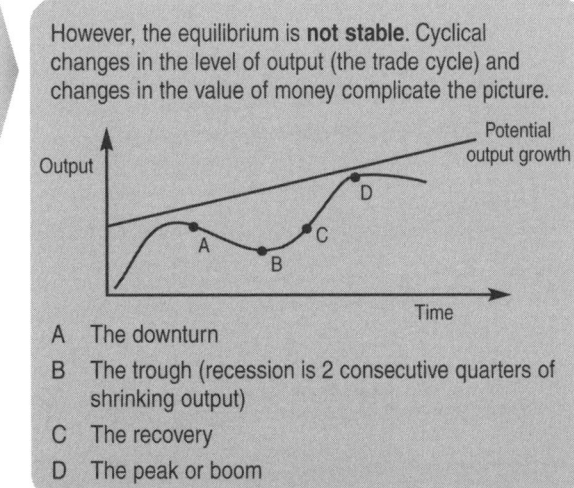

Output

Potential output growth

A

B

C

D

Time

A   The downturn

B   The trough (recession is 2 consecutive quarters of shrinking output)

C   The recovery

D   The peak or boom

1   The elasticity of AS varies from high to zero as output increases because first, less productive resources (especially labour) are brought into use and, second, the limit of potential output is approached.

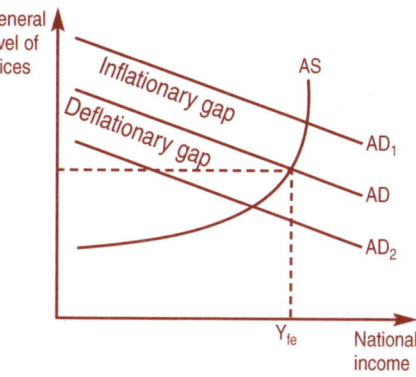

2   AD gives full employment. An increase to AD1 is **inflationary** while a reduction to AD2 is **deflationary.**

3   The inverse relationship between unemployment and inflation is supported by the **Phillips curve** (see Chapter 16).

The depression years

In the 1930s, the global economy contracted even beyond recession into **depression**, with very high unemployment. Traditional economic analysis indicated that the labour market would return to full employment if wage rates fell.

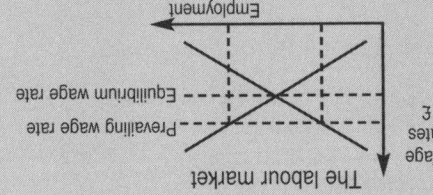

The labour market

This was politically and socially unacceptable. Keynes diagnosed a **deflationary gap** and proposed increases in government spending to shift AD to the right. This would increase national income and reduce unemployment.

Keynes' analysis

Keynes showed that the economy could reach long-term equilibrium at less than full employment.

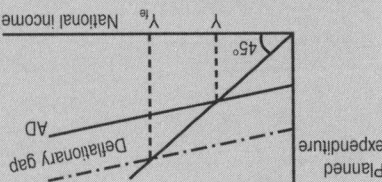

All points on the 45° line represent equilibrium; only one achieves full employment (Y_{fe}). If the AD line is not high enough, a deflationary gap will result.

Analysing aggregate demand

1. **Autonomous** consumption takes place even when national income falls, financed by savings or borrowing.

2. Remaining consumption increases when income increases; the percentage of extra income spent depends on the **marginal propensity to consume** (MPC). The balance percentage is the **marginal propensity to save** (MPS). (Ignoring taxation and imports.) Thus:

$$C = a + bY$$

3. Injections (J) and withdrawals (W) also form part of AD.

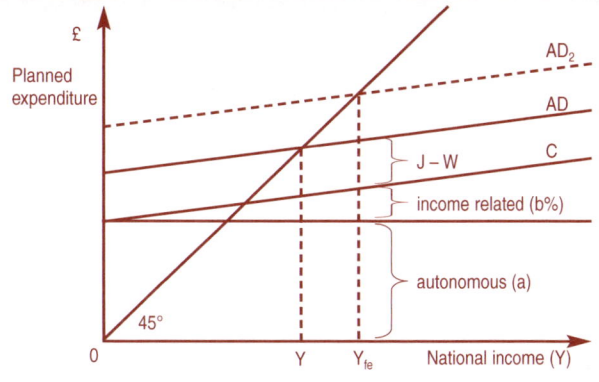

4. If the equilibrium national income Y is less than the full employment level as shown, there is a deflationary gap and AD must be raised to AD_2 to eliminate it.

5. Keynes proposed an increase in J via an increase in government spending financed by borrowing in order to achieve this.

Factors influencing consumption

- The **marginal propensity to consume** is higher among poor households: rich households save more of any increase in disposable income.

- **Income**: the level of present income is clearly important, as may be previous income and social attitudes about income.

- **Wealth**: increases in liquid wealth probably lead to increased consumption.

- **Interest rates**: lower interest rates may encourage spending on credit.

Factors influencing saving

- **Interest rates**: high interest rates may reduce the rate of saving, since the same sum may be obtained with a smaller investment. However, there is some evidence that higher interest rates encourage saving.

- **Distribution of income**: wealthier households have a higher marginal propensity to save than poor households since they have more spare cash.

- **Inflation of asset prices**: people may save in order to maintain their perceived wealth. If the price of marginal assets such as owner occupied housing rises, saving may fall. This is an example of **money illusion**.

Investment is an **injection** into the circular flow and has an important effect on the level of national income.

Productivity-enhancing investment moves the production possibility frontier outwards, thus reducing the inflationary gap potential of increased investment.

The level of investment depends largely on **interest rates** and the degree of **business confidence**.

Interest rates

- The effect of interest rates on overall investment intentions is largely determined by the **marginal efficiency of capital** curve (see Chapter 6)

- Interest rates may also have an effect on the size of the **MPC** and **MPS** and thus affect consumption. This will, in turn, affect business confidence.

Business confidence

- The private sector will invest only if there is a reasonable probability of being able to sell the goods and services eventually produced. When the trade cycle is on the upswing, employment and hence sales expand; in a recession, firms wish to destock and cut costs.

The multiplier

The **multiplier** is the **process of circulation of income** in the national economy, whereby an injection of a certain size leads to a much larger increase in national income. The firms or households receiving the injection use at least part of the money to increase their own consumption. This provides money for other firms and households to repeat the process and so on.

The eventual total increase in national income will be greater in size than the initial increase in expenditure. This is because of the continuing circulation of the funds concerned.

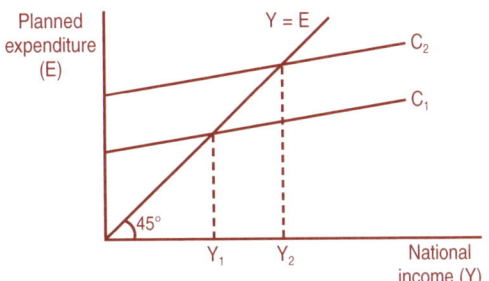

If injections were increased (for example, an increase in government spending or extra exports), there would be a shift upwards in the C curve from C_1 to C_2. Notice that the increase in the level of national income from Y_1 to Y_2 is bigger than the increase in injections. This is the multiplier effect.

$$\text{Multiplier} = \frac{\text{Total increase in national income}}{\text{Initial increase in national income}} = \frac{1}{1-\text{MPC}} = \frac{1}{\text{MPS}}$$

The multiplier also works in reverse

The accelerator

A small percentage change in the output of consumer goods leads to a much larger percentage change in the output of capital goods. Demand for capital goods is divided into replacement units and extra units. Replacement units will be a small percentage of total holdings. An equally small percentage increase in holdings can therefore double total capital purchases. This implies that investment remains high only when consumption is rising.

The accelerator also works in reverse

The Keynesian approach to managing the economy concentrated on AD. Supply side economists believe that AS is at least as important and possibly more so. They suggest that in modern economies, expansion of AD will merely produce inflation and that it is more important for governments to pursue policies that expand AS. This is largely a matter of **deregulation**.

- Labour market regulation, welfare benefits and powerful protected trade unions force wages too high.
- High rates of direct taxation reduce the incentive to work and expand business.
- State controlled industries are inefficient.

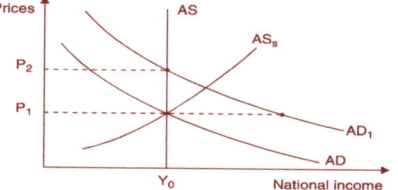

An expansion of AD from AD to AD_1 produces an increase in national income in the short run (AS_S) but in the longer run AS is vertical and inflation results.

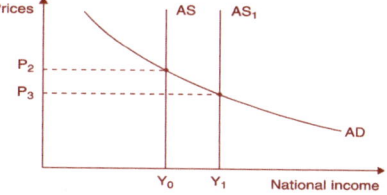

An increase in productive capacity permits a non-inflationary expansion of AS. The increased employment that follows generates extra demand and the economy remains in equilibrium.

15: Money and inflation

Topic List

Theories of money

Inflation

This chapter continues our treatment of money and associated ideas. Monetary theory is an unlikely topic for questions but provides important background. Inflation is an important subject.

Classical quantity theory: *Fisher*

Money is used as a medium of exchange. It is needed only to settle transactions.

$MV \equiv PT$

M = money supply
P = price level
V = velocity of circulation
T = number of transactions

If V and T are roughly constant any increase in M will lead to a rise in P, ie **inflation** since AD will

Liquidity preference theory: *Keynes*

3 motives for holding money:

- Transactions
- Precautionary
- Speculative (to invest if interest rates rise)
  Low interest rates $\Rightarrow$ high liquidity preference
  High interest rates $\Rightarrow$ low liquidity preference

An increase in the money supply leads to a fall in interest rates but only affects AD indirectly.

New quantity theory: *Friedman*

$MV \equiv PQ$ where Q = physical quantity of national output.

An increase in M leads to inflation.

Note. Inflation's effect on money and its functions are dealt with in Chapter 11.

Disadvantages of inflation

- Redistribution of income and wealth from creditors to debtors since debts' real value diminishes
- Impoverishment of those on fixed incomes
- Resource costs of changing prices, eg issue of new price lists
- Reduction in growth of GDP due to uncertainty about costs and in extreme cases (hyperinflation) reluctance to use the currency

Causes of inflation

- **Demand pull** inflation arises when AD is greater than the economy's productive capacity, ie when there is an inflationary gap.
- **Cost push** inflation can occur when costs of factors of production increase even though they are not in short supply. This is particularly apparent in the case of **labour**; strong trade unions can drive up wages even when the economy is underproducing. Import costs are also an important source of inflation.
- **Expectations** of inflation can actually bring it about, when they lead to increased wage demands.
- See also 'Theories of money' above.

Measuring inflation in the UK

RPI is an index of a wide rage of costs.

RPIX excludes mortgage payments from the index.

Notes

Topic List

Unemployment

Unemployment and inflation

Monetary policy

This chapter deals with a very specific aspect of macroeconomic management: the relationship between the money supply and productive capacity.

Categories of unemployment

- **Frictional**: time is required to match job seekers with available vacancies. The unemployment is short-term.

- **Seasonal** unemployment is typical of some industries, such as agriculture and tourism.

- **Structural**: long term changes in an industry reduce the demand for labour. This may be the result of long term decline or technology-based productivity improvements.

- **Cyclical** or **demand deficient**: during the downswing of the trade cycle, AD contracts and there is a deflationary gap. Output and employment both fall.

Consequences of unemployment

- Loss of output
- Loss of 'human capital', ie skills
- Increasing income inequalities
- Social costs such as mental health problems, divorce and crime
- Effect on government finances of increased welfare payments

Calculating unemployment

$$\frac{\text{Number unemployed}}{\text{Total workforce}} \times 100\%$$

Both quantities are subject to statistical errors and political massage.

The Phillips curve

AW Phillips' original study related UK unemployment rates to wage growth rates for the years 1861 to 1957. The curve appeared to confirm the Keynesian theory of a link between unemployment and inflation and to offer governments a simple trade-off: unemployment can be reduced at the cost of increasing inflation, by stimulating aggregate demand.

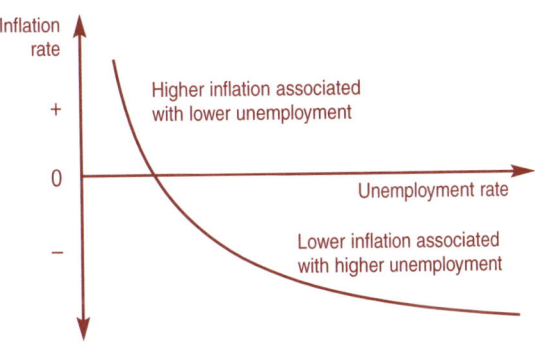

Stagflation In the UK, the Phillips curve relationship broke down at the end of the 1960s, when both inflation and unemployment rose.

16: Monetary policy, unemployment and inflation

Refining the Phillips curve

- **Structural** and **frictional** unemployment are unlikely to be affected by a rise in AD: only **demand-deficient** unemployment will fall.

- Non-labour cost push inflation complicates the relationship.

- **Inflationary expectations** are incorporated into wage bargaining and the short-run Phillips curve shifts upwards. The long run curve is vertical at the **non-accelerating inflation rate of unemployment**. The only effective way to reduce NAIRU is to use **supply side measures** to make the labour market less rigid. This implies reducing trade union power.

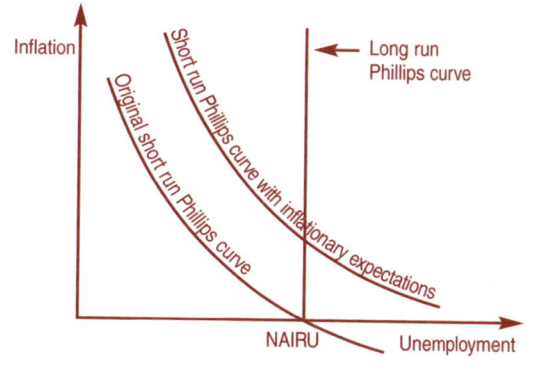

Monetary policy is concerned with the quantity and value of money in the economy; that is with the money supply, inflation, interest rates and exchange rates.

In the past, monetary policy has had a variety of targets.

- **The exchange rate**: a stable exchange rate has been seen as of primary importance for a trading nation. Very high interest rates have occasionally been required to maintain a fixed exchange rate, with undesirable consequences for economic growth.

- **The money supply** has been targeted in an attempt to control inflation. This policy broke down, partly because of the difficulty of defining a suitable monetary aggregate, and partly because the link with inflation is questionable.

- **Interest rates**: cheap borrowing encourages spending and thus increase national income by expanding both investment and AD. However, easy credit trends to suck in imported consumer goods, thus harming the balance of trade. Attempts have been made to confine the desirable effect of low interest rates to industry, but they do not work.

- **Inflation** was a major problem until recently and is still the main target of monetary policy in the UK. Other western governments use monetary policy to balance inflation and growth, but the UK seems particularly prone to inflation.

16: Monetary policy, unemployment and inflation

In the UK, the Bank of England implements the government's monetary policy. Various techniques have been used, all aimed at controlling the bank's ability to create credit.

- **Directives**, formal or informal, to the clearing banks on credit creation are no longer used.

- **Monetary base** controls can be implemented by requiring the banks to maintain specific asset ratios or by **open market operations**. The latter tends to make exchange rates unstable.

- **Special deposits** with the Bank of England have sometimes been called for. Like directives, such schemes limit the banks competitiveness and are of limited effectiveness.

- **Interest rates** have been controlled by the Bank's Monetary Policy Committee since 1997. The MPC is responsible for attaining the government's inflation target of 2½% pa.

Open market operations

The Bank buys and sells large quantities of government bills every day. The net cash movement influences the monetary base. The prices at which it buys and sells effectively set the basis for the banks' interest rate structure.

Example

If one pays £91 for a £100 nominal value 5% bill, one receives £5 income pa on an investment of £91. This is equivalent to an interest rate of 5½%.

17: Fiscal policy and taxation

Topic List

Fiscal policy

Taxation

This chapter completes our coverage of macroeconomic fundamentals. Be aware that many questions will require you to draw on knowledge of both monetary and fiscal matters, especially where the objectives of government policy are concerned.

A government's fiscal policy is concerned with its plans for taxation, borrowing and spending. It is an important part of its macroeconomic management.

Automatic stabilisers

reduce the value of the **multiplier**, thus dampening both expansion and contraction.

- Most tax revenues rise as national income rises and vice versa
- Welfare payments fall as national income rises and vice versa

The effect of G and T on AD is thus reduced.

Crowding out

occurs when government spending merely replaces private spending. This is likely when the government borrows to spend unless there really are plentiful **idle resources** such as high unemployment.

Fiscal policies

Taxation (T) is a **withdrawal** and government spending (G) is an **injection**.

- **Expansionary fiscal stance**: G > T; there is a public sector net cash requirement (PSNCR) so borrowing increases the national debt. Used in recession to expand AD and reduce unemployment.

- **Contractionary fiscal stance**: T > G; national debt reduced by public sector debt repayment. Used to control demand-pull inflation when AD is too high.

- **Neutral fiscal stance**: T = G. However if T and G rise by the same amount, AD expands, since households would have saved some of the money they pay in extra tax, but the government spends all of it. This is the **balanced budget multiplier**.

Functions of taxation

- Raise revenue for government
- Discourage some consumption (eg smoking)
- Align purchase costs with social costs (eg landfill tax on 'active waste')
- Redistribute income and wealth
- Protect industry against foreign competition
- Stabilise national income via fiscal stance

Qualities of a good tax (*Adam Smith*)

- **Equity**: people should pay according to their ability.
- **Certainty**: taxpayers must know what is expected of them.
- **Convenience**: payment should be related to occasions of income and expenditure (eg PAYE and VAT).
- **Economy**: costs of collection should be small relative to the yield.

Other desirable features

- **Flexibility**: it should be possible to adjust rates up or down.
- **Efficiency**: it should achieve its aim and not encourage evasion or avoidance.

Direct taxes are paid directly by the taxpayer to the Exchequer (eg income tax).

Indirect taxes are collected from an intermediary who passes it on (eg VAT).

Direct taxes (eg income tax) are usually **progressive.**

Indirect taxes (eg VAT) are normally **regressive.**

- A **regressive tax** takes a higher proportion of a poor person's salary than of a rich person's (eg license fees for cars).
- A **progressive tax** takes a higher proportion of a rich person's income than of a poor person's (eg income tax with basic and higher rates).
- A **proportional tax** takes the same proportion of income from everybody.

17: Fiscal policy and taxation

Progressive direct taxes

- Equitable economic, convenient and certain
- Act as automatic stabilisers
- Enable redistribution of wealth
- High levels deter enterprise, encourage avoidance
- High rates can reduce revenue (the Laffer curve)

Indirect taxes

- Almost inevitably regressive
- Contribute to inflation
- Convenient, may be economic, not equitable or certain
- Encourage the 'black economy'
- Can be used to encourage/discourage certain products

18: International trade

Topic List

Globalisation

International trade

Free trade agreements

This chapter and the next deal with international aspects of economics. This is a very large field and provides ample material for questions.

Multinational companies (MNCs)

operate in more than one country, rather than just trading internationally. Ownership or control of a production or service facility in another country is the test. Major MNCs such as Ford have turnover greater than the GNP of small countries.

International trade

is regulated by a complex system of bilateral, multilateral, regional and global agreements. The World Trade Organisation promotes global agreements.

MNCs and globalisation of trade

Reasons for multinational operations

- **Cost advantage**: reduce cost of transport to final market by manufacturing locally; exploit availability of cheap labour

- **Expand by horizontal integration**: access markets protected by tariffs; seek economies of scale from increased turnover

- **Local market requirements**: satisfy by local manufacturing and distribution

Global financial markets

Improved IT systems and deregulation of markets mean capital can be moved rapidly around the world in order to achieve the best returns.

MNCs and the national economy

- MNCs may import **capital**, thus expanding potential GNP. Even where local capital is used, they may mobilise it better

- MNCs may **transfer technology**, again expanding potential GNP

- MNCs will bring advanced **management practices** and **IT systems**

- MNCs may exploit different tax systems, using **transfer pricing** to declare profits in countries where they pay least tax

- **Remission of profits** out of the country is a withdrawal from the circular flow

- MNCs may require **subsidies** or **tax privileges** before establishing operations

Absolute advantage

A country has an absolute advantage over another when it is **more efficient** in the production of a given good; ie, when it can **produce more with the same resources.**

Comparative advantage

A country has a comparative advantage over another when it can produce a given good at a **lower opportunity cost**; ie production of another good given. Comparative advantage makes trade advantageous.

Other advantages of free trade

- Matching surpluses and deficits of **raw materials**
- Increased **competition** improves products and drives down prices
- Larger markets lead to **economies of scale**
- Development of political and social links

Example

Country X and country Y produce lorries and wheat in the quantities given below. Each uses the same quantity of resources in total.

	Lorries	Wheat (tons)
X	20	200
Y	10	150

Country X must give up 10 tons of wheat to obtain 1 lorry while Y must give up 15. However, X must give up 1/10 lorry for 1 ton of wheat while Y loses only 1/15.

X has comparative advantage in lorries.
Y has comparative advantage in wheat.

X has an absolute advantage in the production of both lorries and wheat.

Both will benefit from trade and specialisation.

Arguments for protection

- **Employment protection**: cheap imports from low wage countries mean domestic industries cannot compete. Business failure and unemployment ensue.
- **Balance of payments**: imports must be financed or the exchange rate will be driven down (see Chapter 19). Restricting imports reduces the pressure.
- **Infant industries**: less developed countries need to assist their developing industries to become established.
- **Unfair trade practices**: exporters may sell at less than cost ('dumping') to gain a foothold; governments may subsidise exports.
- **Revenue**: tariffs raise revenue painlessly.
- **Strategic industries**: some industries (defence, agriculture) are favoured for strategic reasons.

Arguments against protection

- **Reduction in welfare**: protection reduces global trade and hence global production.
- **Inefficiency**: domestic industries become inefficient through lack of competition. Also, declining industries linger and new ones are hampered.
- **Higher prices**: cheap imports reduce the cost of living.
- **Retaliation**: retaliatory response by other countries is likely to harm the domestic economy.

European Union

The European Union (EU) combines a free trade area with a customs union and a common market. The aim is complete freedom of trade, including free movement of capital and labour and no national preference in the award of public sector contracts. However, barriers still exist in the form of different tax systems, infrastructure, skill levels and prosperity.

The **European Economic Area** links the EU to Norway and Iceland.

North American Free Trade Agreement

The North American Free Trade Agreement links Mexico, the USA and Canada in a free trade area.

Aims of World Trade Organisation

- Reduce barriers to free trade
- Eliminate discrimination in trade
- Deter protectionist measures

Free trade area: no restrictions on the supply of goods and services.

Customs union: a free trade area with common external tariffs on imports from non-member countries.

Common market: a customs union with free movement of factors of production: this may lead to harmonisation of economic policy, taxation and commercial law; and political co-operation.

19: The balance of payments

Topic List

The balance of payments

The terms of trade

Exchange rates

This chapter completes both our coverage of international trade economics and these Passcards. Be aware that the balance of payments and the exchange rate are topics that are both linked to one another and also linked to the whole area of macroeconomic policy in general and monetary policy in particular.

A country's balance of payments is a statement of the value of its transactions with other countries.

Used to be called 'visible trade'

Profits, dividends, interest, wages and salaries

Includes foreign aid, payments to EU and UN and individual deposits

Movement in fixed assets

Transfer of ownership of businesses, bonds and shares

Samples are used rather than 100% record of transactions

UK balance of payments 1999 (net amounts)

	£bn
Current account	
Trade in goods	−26,767
Trade in services	11,538
Income	8,332
Transfers	−4,084
Current balance	−10,981
Capital account	776
Financial account	5,853
Net errors and omissions	4,352
	0

The UK always imports more goods than it sells overseas, but normally has a surplus on services.

The balance of payments is a double entry system: it must sum to zero.

> A country's terms of trade show the quantity of domestic goods it must export in order to pay for the goods it imports.

The terms of trade are an export:import price ratio. If the world price for a country's export falls relative to that of its imports, its terms of trade will deteriorate, and vice versa.

Changes in the terms of trade are particularly important. The annual charge is computed as:

$$\frac{\text{Price of exports in year 1} \div \text{price of exports in year 2}}{\text{Price of imports in year 1} \div \text{price of imports in year 2}}$$

The significance of the terms of trade

1 Primary sector outputs such as minerals and agricultural products are subject to major fluctuations on world commodity markets. Lesser developed countries tend to rely on the export of a few such products. A fall in the price of exports can have a major effect on the development of such countries' economies.

2 The effect of changes in the terms of trade depends on the **elasticities of demand** of imports and exports; eg a rise in the terms of trade will produce a balance of deficit if export demand is highly elastic and import demand is highly inelastic.

A currency's exchange rate is its value in terms of another currency.

Fixed exchange rates

facilitate trade. They may be set in terms of gold or a **reserve currency** such as the US dollar. Countries may have to buy their own currency, using **official reserves** of gold and other currencies in order to maintain a fixed exchange rate. The 19th century **gold standard** and the post-World War II **Bretton Woods** system were fixed exchange rate systems.

Floating exchange rates

Most currencies in the developed world have free floating exchange rates – they are determined by supply and demand. All the transactions listed in the balance of payments contribute to the exchange rate since they imply the purchase or sale of the home currency. **Trade** and short-term **investment** are two very important influences, the latter being heavily influenced by **interest rates** (high interest rates attract investment which increases demand for the currency so the exchange rate rises).

A 'dirty float' occurs when a central bank buys or sells its own currency in order to achieve an unofficial target rate.

The exchange rate and the balance of payments

A deterioration in the balance of trade may put downward pressure on the exchange rate, unless capital flows can compensate.

A falling exchange rate makes imports more expensive and exports cheaper. It can therefore help to restore a trade deficit. However, the initial inelasticity of demand of both imports and exports means that the trade deficit is likely to worsen in the short term. This is the **J curve effect**.

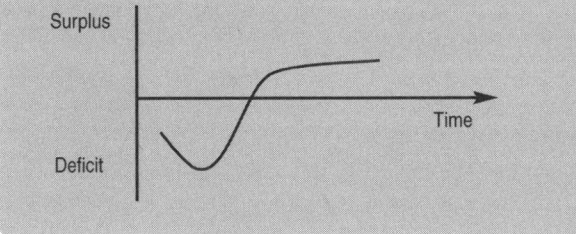

The foreign exchange market

London has the world's largest foreign exchange market. Individual dealers within the commercial banks communicate with one another electronically, buying and selling currencies and thus setting market prices.

Spot transactions are settled within 2 days.

Forward transactions guarantee a certain rate at some point in the future.

Speculation by dealers can have a significant effect on an exchange rate, especially if it is seen to be overvalued.

High inflation will weaken a country's exchange rate in response to the overall fall in the value of the currency.

European monetary union

Membership:	All EU countries except UK and Denmark
Start date:	1 January 1999 - creation of the euro as a currency
Notes and coins:	Available from 1 January 2002 (electronic transfers and credit transfers before this date)
Bank:	European Central Bank (ECB), Wim Duisenberg, President

Important aspects of EMU

- A **single monetary policy** managed by the ECB and aimed at achieving price stability.
- Member countries must not use **fiscal policy** to circumvent ECB monetary policy.
- **Trade** should expand within the EU as currency risk and transaction costs are removed.
- Pricing policies will become **transparent** across the EU.

- EMU depends on treating the whole of the EU as **one economic unit**. It is feared that a single monetary policy and co-ordinated fiscal policies might not be suitable for some areas, leading to prolonged local recessions.
- **Seigneurage**: if the EU is purchased as a reserve currency, that extra demand may allow interest rates to be lowered.

19: The balance of payments

Notes